Fire

Applewood Books
Carlisle, Massachusetts

978-1-4290-9411-5

To inquire about this edition
or to request a free copy
of our current catalog
featuring our best-selling books, write to:
Applewood Books
P.O. Box 27
Carlisle, MA 01741
For more complete listings,
visit us on the web at:
www.awb.com

10 9 8 7 6 5 4 3 2 1
MANUFACTURED IN THE UNITED STATES OF AMERICA

Fire is a potent symbol for life and inspiration, death and rebirth. Unlike any other element, fire 'breathes' oxygen and 'eats' wood, vegetation, almost everything in its path; it grows, births new fires; it excretes ash. Is it any wonder that fire has worked for centuries as a powerful metaphor for life?

The fire's spark has long been equated with the birth of ideas, inspiration, awakening. This volume of quotations is populated with many such examples. The spark of passion is one of the most common fire metaphors. And it is deeply appropriate when you contemplate the nature of passion and its ability to kindle love and consume hearts. In a 1954 interview, actress Joan Crawford famously said, "Love is a fire. But whether it is going to warm your hearth or burn down your house, you can never tell." This, of course, is a modern take on old wisdom from Aesop's *Fables* that states: "It is with our passions as it is with fire and water; they are good servants, but bad masters."

Fire, like water, is a necessary but dangerous force, and not easily controlled. At its most dangerous, fire will destroy all. But it also holds the possibility of purification and rebirth. Think, for instance, of the mythical phoenix as described by Janet Fitch: "The phoenix must burn to emerge."

—Applewood Books

"The mind is not a vessel to be filled but a fire to be kindled."

—Plutarch

"In the silence of love
You will find the spark of life."

—Rumi

"Fire is always ready to burn the hand it warms."

—Rachel Caine

"The heart is an organ of fire."

—Michael Ondaatje

"Fire may be represented as the destroyer of all sophistry, and as the image and demonstration of truth; because it is light and drives out darkness which conceals all essences [or subtle things]."

—Leonardo da Vinci

"Bee to the blossom, moth to the flame; each to his passion; what's in a name?"

—Helen Hunt Jackson

"To learn to read is to light a fire; every syllable that is spelled out is a spark."

—Victor Hugo

"Just as a candle cannot burn without fire, men cannot live without a spiritual life."

—Buddha

"Fire is such a fragile and beautiful thing. People think it's a manly thing—fire and you burn things. But it's, on the contrary, very feminine. It's very fragile. I love it."

—Chef Francis Mallmann

"Fire is the most tolerable third party."

—Henry David Thoreau

"Even in a time of elephantine vanity and greed, one never has to look far to see the campfires of gentle people."

—Garrison Keillor

"I can't give you the white picket fence, and if I did, you'd set it on fire."

—Ilona Andrews

"A heart well worth winning, and well won. A heart that, once won, goes through fire and water for the winner, and never changes, and is never daunted."

—Charles Dickens

"We each have a special something we can get only at a special time of our life. Like a small flame. A careful, fortunate few cherish that flame, nurture it, hold it as a torch to light their way. But once that flame goes out, it's gone forever."

—Haruki Murakami

"Every idea is an incitement.... Eloquence may set fire to reason."

—Oliver Wendell Holmes

"Ladybug ladybug fly away home,
Your house in on fire and your children are gone."

—Traditional nursery rhyme

"You can blow out a candle
But you can't blow out a fire
Once the flames begin to catch
The wind will blow it higher."

—Peter Gabriel

"Nature teaches more than she preaches. There are no sermons in stones. It is easier to get a spark out of a stone than a moral."

—John Burroughs

"Love is a fire. But whether it is going to warm your hearth or burn down your house, you can never tell."

—Joan Crawford

"But denunciatory rhetoric is so much easier and cheaper than good works, and proves a popular temptation. Yet is it far better to light the candle than to curse the darkness."

—William Lonsdale Watkinson

"While I was looking the other way your fire
went out
Left me with cinders to kick into dust
What a waste of the wonder you were
In my living fire I will keep your scorn and mine
In my living fire I will keep your heartache and
mine
At the disgrace of a waste of a life."

—Kristin Cashore

"A book, too, can be a star, a living fire to lighten the darkness, leading out into the expanding universe."

—Madeleine L'Engle

"The most powerful weapon on earth is the human soul on fire."

—Marshal Ferdinand Foch

"Hate is like fire; it burns those who hold it."

—Alden Loveshade

"There is no fire like passion, there is no shark like hatred, there is no snare like folly, there is no torrent like greed."

—Buddha

"It's too bad if a heart lacks fire,
and is deprived of the light of a heart ablaze.
The day on which you are
without passionate love
is the most wasted day of your life."

—Omar Khayyam

"As soon go kindle fire with snow, as seek to quench the fire of love with words."

—William Shakespeare

"Grilling, broiling, barbecuing—whatever you want to call it—is an art, not just a matter of building a pyre and throwing on a piece of meat as a sacrifice to the gods of the stomach."

—James Beard

"Each separate dying ember wrought its ghost upon the floor."

—Edgar Allan Poe

"Love is the Fire of Life; it either consumes or purifies."

—Swedish proverb

"The most tangible of all visible mysteries—fire."

—Leigh Hunt

"He who sits by the fire, thankless for the fire, is just as if he had no fire. Nothing is possessed save in appreciation, of which thankfulness is the indispensable ingredient."

—W. J. Cameron

"In my biology class, we'd talked about the definition of life: to be classified as a living creature, a thing needs to eat, breathe, reproduce, and grow.... Fire, by that definition, is vibrantly alive. It eats everything from wood to flesh, excreting the waste as ash, and it breathes air just like a human, taking in oxygen and emitting carbon. Fire grows, and as it spreads, it creates new fires that spread out and make new fires of their own. Fire drinks gasoline and excretes cinders, it fights for territory, it loves and hates. Sometimes when I watch people trudging through their daily routines, I think that fire is more alive than we are—brighter, hotter, more sure of itself and where it wants to go. Fire doesn't settle; fire doesn't tolerate; fire doesn't 'get by.'
Fire does.
Fire is."

—Dan Wells

"You're only given a little spark of madness. You mustn't lose it."

—Robin Williams

"Each of us is born with a box of matches inside us but we can't strike them all by ourselves."

—Laura Esquivel

"How is it that one match can start a forest fire, but it takes a whole box of matches to start a campfire?"

—Christy Whitehead

"Burn me down to ashes,
Lend me to the flames.
Rise again I valiantly shall,
For LOVE is but my name."

—Anurag Anand

"It was a pleasure to burn. It was a special pleasure to see things eaten, to see things blackened and changed. With the brass nozzle in his fists, with this great python spitting its venomous kerosene upon the world, the blood pounded in his head, and his hands were the hands of some amazing conductor playing all the symphonies of blazing and burning to bring down the tatters and charcoal ruin of history. With his symbolic helmet numbered 451 on his stolid head, and his eyes all orange flame with the thought of what came next, he flicked the igniter and the house jumped up in a gorging fire that burned the evening sky red and yellow and black. He strode in a swarm of fireflies. He wanted above all, like the old joke, to shove a marshmallow on a stick in the furnace, while the flapping pigeon-winged books died on the porch and lawn of the house. While the books went up in sparkling whirls and blew away on a wind turned dark with burning."

—Ray Bradbury

"Earth, water, fire, and wind. Where there is energy there is life."

—Suzy Kassem

"Honest criticism means nothing: what one wants is unrestrained passion, fire for fire."

—Henry Miller

"The point about hope is that it is something that occurs in very dark moments. It is like a flame in the darkness; it isn't like a confidence and promise."

—John Berger

"We all live in a house on fire, no fire department to call; no way out, just the upstairs window to look out of while the fire burns the house down with us trapped, locked in it."

—Tennessee Williams

"Motivation is a fire from within. If someone else tries to light that fire under you, chances are it will burn very briefly."

—Stephen R. Covey

"The phoenix must burn to emerge."

—Janet Fitch

"Love is like a friendship caught on fire. In the beginning a flame, very pretty, often hot and fierce, but still only light and flickering. As love grows older, our hearts mature and our love becomes as coals, deep-burning and unquenchable."

—Bruce Lee

"The moon's an arrant thief,
And her pale fire she snatches from the sun."

—William Shakespeare

"Move swift as the Wind and closely-formed as
the Wood.
Attack like the Fire and be still as the Mountain."

—Sun Tzu

"It is with our passions as it is with fire and water; they are good servants, but bad masters."

—Aesop

"There is an electric fire in human nature tending to purify—so that among these human creatures there is continually some birth of new heroism. The pity is that we must wonder at it, as we should at finding a pearl in rubbish."

—John Keats

"It is not light that we need, but fire; it is not the gentle shower, but thunder. We need the storm, the whirlwind, and the earthquake."

—Frederick Douglass

"The fire is the main comfort of the camp, whether in summer or winter, and is about as ample at one season as at another. It is as well for cheerfulness as for warmth and dryness."

—Henry David Thoreau

"Since the house is on fire let us warm ourselves."

—Italian proverb

"One can enjoy a wood fire worthily only when he warms his thoughts by it as well as hands and feet."

—Odell Shepard

"Among the notable things about fire is that it also requires oxygen to burn—exactly like its enemy, life. Thereby are life and flames so often compared."

—Otto Weininger

"The Sun, the hearth of affection and life, pours burning love on the delighted earth."

—Arthur Rimbaud

"A woodland in full color is awesome as a forest fire, in magnitude at least, but a single tree is like a dancing tongue of flame to warm the heart."

—Hal Borland

"Time is the substance from which I am made. Time is a river which carries me along, but I am the river; it is a tiger that devours me, but I am the tiger; it is a fire that consumes me, but I am the fire."

—Jorge Luis Borges

"It's best to have failure happen early in life. It wakes up the Phoenix bird in you so you rise from the ashes."

—Anne Baxter

"Come Fairies, take me out of this dull world, for I would ride with you upon the wind and dance upon the mountains like a flame!"

—William Butler Yeats

"To bring the dead to life
is no great magic.
Few are wholly dead:
Blow on a dead man's embers
And a live flame will start."

—Robert Graves

"Neither fire nor wind, birth nor death can erase our good deeds."

—Buddha

"Even if there is only one possible unified theory, it is just a set of rules and equations. What is it that breathes fire into the equations and makes a universe for them to describe?"

—Stephen Hawking

"A house is not a home unless it contains food and fire for the mind as well as the body."

—Benjamin Franklin

"I hold with those who favor fire.
But if it had to perish twice,
I think I know enough of hate
To know that for destruction ice
Is also great."

—Robert Frost

"Words are only painted fire; a look is the fire itself."

—Mark Twain

"Fire is the test of gold; adversity, of strong men."

—Martha Graham

"Labor to keep alive in your breast that little spark of celestial fire, called conscience."

—George Washington

"Fire has always been and, seemingly, will always remain, the most terrible of the elements."

—Harry Houdini

"Leaders should lead as far as they can and then vanish. Their ashes should not choke the fire they have lit."

—H. G. Wells

"Music should strike fire from the heart of man, and bring tears from the eyes of woman."

—Ludwig van Beethoven

"Life is a flame that is always burning itself out, but it catches fire again every time a child is born."

—George Bernard Shaw

"Civilization did not come with fire. It came with the discovery of how to use fire to heat water."

—Laura Anne Gilman

"Where such forest lands have been protected from fire, as they are very largely through the progress of settlement, young trees have usually sprung up in great numbers under or between the scattered veterans which had survived the fires, and a dense and vigorous young growth stands ready to replace, by a heavy forest, the open park-like condition which the fire had created and maintained..."

—Gifford Pinchot

"The finest steel has to go through the hottest fire."

—Richard M. Nixon

"There may be a great fire in our soul, yet no one ever comes to warm himself at it, and the passers-by see only a wisp of smoke."

—Vincent van Gogh

"The weakest of all weak things is a virtue that has not been tested in the fire."

—Mark Twain

"Absence diminishes small loves and increases great ones, as the wind blows out the candle and fans the bonfire."

—François de la Rochefoucauld

"Joy is the holy fire that keeps our purpose warm and our intelligence aglow."

—Helen Keller

"A spark neglected makes a mighty fire."

—Robert Herrick

"May you always have walls for the winds, a roof for the rain, tea beside the fire, laughter to cheer you, those you love near you and all your heart might desire."

—Irish blessing

"The one advantage of playing with fire, Lady Caroline, is that one never gets even singed. It is the people who don't know how to play with it who get burned up."

—Oscar Wilde

"Your own property is concerned when your neighbor's house is on fire."

—Horace

"Time is the school in which we learn,
Time is the fire in which we burn."

—Delmore Schwartz

"She's mad, but she's magic. There's no lie in her fire."

—Charles Bukowski

"The very existence of flame-throwers proves that some time, somewhere, someone said to themselves, 'You know, I want to set those people over there on fire, but I'm just not close enough to get the job done.'"

—George Carlin

"Fan the sinking flame of hilarity with the wing of friendship; and pass the rosy wine."

—Charles Dickens

"I would mould a world of fire and dew."

—William Butler Yeats

"The world's flattery and hypocrisy is a sweet morsel: eat less of it, for it is full of fire.
Its fire is hidden while its taste is manifest,
but its smoke becomes visible in the end."

—Rumi

"A woman would run through fire and water for such a kind heart."

—William Shakespeare

"The fireworks begin today. Each diploma is a lighted match. Each one of you is a fuse."

—Ed Koch

"One thing that's great about firefighters: If they don't have the equipment they desperately need, they don't have the help, they don't care. They'll do it on their own."

—Denis Leary

"Bitterness is like cancer. It eats upon the host. But anger is like fire. It burns it all clean."

—Maya Angelou

"Remember, only you can prevent wildfires."

—Smokey Bear

"I have no ambition in this world but one
and that is to be a fireman.
The position may in the eyes of some
appear to be a lowly one;
But those who know the work
which a fireman has to do
believe his is a noble calling.
Our proudest moment is to save...lives.
Under the impulse of such thoughts
the nobility of the occupation
thrills us and stimulates us
to deeds of daring
even of supreme sacrifice."

—Edward F. Croker

"Some say the world will end in fire, some say in ice."

—Robert Frost

"They say a good love is one that sits you down, gives you a drink of water, and pats you on top of the head. But I say a good love is one that casts you into the wind, sets you ablaze, makes you burn through the skies and ignite the night like a phoenix; the kind that cuts you loose like a wildfire and you can't stop running simply because you keep on burning everything you touch! I say that's a good love; one that burns and flies, and you run with it."

—C. JoyBell C.

"In everyone's life, at some point, our inner fire goes out. It is then burst into flame by an encounter with another human being. We should all be thankful for those people who rekindle the inner spirit."

—Albert Schweitzer

"To poke a wood fire is more solid enjoyment than almost anything else in the world."

—Charles Dudley Warner

"The five critical tools of game management are the ax, the match, the cow, the plow, and the gun."

—Aldo Leopold

"O joy! That in our embers is something that doth live."

—William Wordsworth